AF209707

ASPECTS OF AGEING

A SUITE OF POEMS ON THE THEMES OF

BODY, MIND AND SPIRIT

IN THE CONTEXT OF MORTALITY

SEÁN GAFFNEY

SECOND EDITION 2020

© 2020 FREEDOM XPRESS

Developed and published by Freedom Xpress, a subdivision of
Lars Berg Egenart

Cover graphic art: Lars Berg.
Graphic design and graphite drawings: Lars Berg.
First published as an eBook/PDF file, now in its second edition
and sold at the Freedom Xpress website.
This is the first printed version of the second edition 2020.
Print: BoD, Sweden 2020.

ISBN 978-91-519-7408-8

For more information on Freedom Xpress
Email: lars@egenart.info
Website: www.freedomxpress.net

Or write to

Lars Berg Egenart
Plogvägen 21
SE-646 34 Gnesta
Sweden

All Souls' Day

I light a candle for each of you:
My granddad, my father and my son.

You, granddad, thought I could be your son
Heard in my voice your dead son's echo…

You, my father, just never knew how to be one
Hoped you could be one if I became your son.

And you, my son, hoped I would be your father.
And now I'm learning how to be your son.

I stand here last of our four generations
Alive in the lives of you, my special dead.

Preface to second edition

My non-professional writing is unplanned and unstructured. So much so that my titles first appear during and/or after the writing, so that possible titles for individual pieces or even suites are not chiselled in stone until the stone is being raised or maybe even standing. For the first time, what I thought was a raised and inscribed stone was still being written on – and I was still the writer!

Clearly, my new pieces were connected backwards to the original suite – and even forwards to my death and its earthly aftermath. Since all my poetry is grounded in my experience, including my memory of past events as a present experience, then my dying is clearly not yet an experience and its aftermath a mystery to me **now** with no longer a me **then** to reflect back on and write about.

So having as usual sent each piece to Lars, illustrator and designer of all my suites and also publisher of the most recent two this one included – I proposed a second edition with a defined *PROLOGUE*, and an *EPILOGUE* to cover the new material.

Seán Gaffney
Stockholm, August 2020

Introduction
To the suite and to my writing

This suite began as I found myself pondering the existential implications of having been through a series of ambulance journeys to my local Accident & Emergency department culminating in a 4-hour surgery under local anaesthetic to my carotid artery. My mortality had been a theme for me – yet again, and more reminders were to come. I was aware that the theme of mortality in general and my own in particular were and are still core to my first two published suites and borrowed the final piece from each as a bridge to and starting block for what was emerging in me as a dedicated suite where my mortality would be core rather than incidental. Little did I know how core it was about to become – and to even touch upon the mystery of immortality...

This introduction ends with a stand-alone piece which says something about my writing and my relationship with you, my possible reader:

My sounds of music

Ba-Ba-Ba BabaBarock:

I heard it on the radio:
Arcangelo Corelli's ornaments:
He wrote them to be played "just so",
He left no room for any arguments.

Ba-Ba-Ba BaBaBaroque,

Beethoven did it his way, well, how else?
His local quartet trying out his latest with him
Hearing what he wrote, his deaf ears silent or
Buzzing with strange noises, now hearing with his eyes:

He liked the variation played by the lead, the fingering
Seen and heard, listening through his eagle eyes,
And changed his score to write it in, anyway now his.
There still, still played I do believe, and hear.

Roll over Beethoven...

And so to jazz, another musical love of mine.
Miles Davis gave bare bones, left it to his soloists to
Ornament them into life, the bars agreed: Coltrane of course
Lost wonderfully in his energised meanderings

Had challenges ending, stayed in his groove
As long as his groove was there, his open, open groove...
Miles "Corelli" offered a solution:
"Ever thought of just taking the horn outa your mouth, man."

And all that jazz.

My writing is all ornament, improv on improv, the melody
    emerging:
Corelli in reverse perhaps, Beethoven changing his score as he
    hears it playing,
Gaffney in his groove: what you see is what I have inside me
    waiting:
My opening lines here up to Ludwig intact from the early 80's...

They unlocked the door of my mind from the inside a week ago
    then
Busking freely day by day, and night by night, this melody
    emerging
And being sung now finally that I've owned my voice:
So thank you Miles and Trane: structure and process meeting...

I had thought that maybe music was my theme, sounds jostling
    in a cacophanous queue
Of worthy figures of the foreground/background noise: the
    most energised of them
Will return I know and sing in me as they need to, though not
    just now it seems:
Now, writing is my theme, how structure emerges from and of
    the process of my writing.

Must ask Iréne and Lasse how it is for them with painting, and
    Lasse sculpts I know:
His wooden shapes I'm sure emerging from his meeting with
    the wood.
Too shy I'd say to reference... was it Michaelangelo?: the figure
    waiting there to be
Discovered, revealed, the figure there already in the block of
    marble or of wood, waiting.

A shaved off piece of wood evoking absence also, and absence is
    of course also a word:
So back to language, my medium: the figure here already in the
    ground of words
Improv seeding improv in a network of connections from which
    new themes emerge
Already waiting there as seeds or shoots even, seeking the nour-
    ishment of light and

Hand in hand or arm in arm, as we may be if you're reading this
   in print, a recording of
This the live performance – even a reading would for me be live
   at one remove. You're
Here now with me, in my mind and index finger as I'm writing,
   now that I've named and
Acknowledged your presence and your influence, no turning
   back, a presence now

Here with me as I write, an echo with opinions, a quartet leader
   doing his own thing so
Back with music I suppose, back where I started, and the
   sounds still here with me still
Queueing, jostling to be heard, asking me for words and
   rhythms to give them life on this
Two dimensional screen and maybe page, words emerging from
   the echoes of music and

Music again through my stanzas of words, the figure in the mar-
   ble, the form in the wood
Sounds still coming, queuing, jostling to be heard: First out:
   Vivaldi's Gloria:
Baroque orchestra, choir and voice, and what a voice: Sara Min-
   gardo and what a
Combination, Sara Mingardo and Vivaldi. Their Qui sedes ad
   dexteram patris, you tube it

Go on: you tube it: just listen to what Vivaldi and Mingardo do
   to the word miserere and
Continue wonderfully to hear it on and on until the firm soft
   "nobis" says "we're done".
And could I ever put that into words, my medium: I 've pon-
   dered it so let me try: from
Word to music, just like miserere as expressed by Vivaldi and
   Mingardo: my word is

Lino, my music is linoleum. Apparently, they mean the same...
   but listen now, just listen:
Lino the hard sharp "i", the matter-of-fact shortness of the
   word, and then linoleum
Thin wispy "i" in lin, expanding lengthening broadening broad-
   ening lengthening in the
Rolling roundness of oleum, prolonged by the generous "m":
   lino to linoleum: I can hear

Mingardo singing, her assured phrasing, the special timbre of
   her voice, her easy
Familiarity with the music and musicians, all there in the whole-
   ness of her singing as the
Figure emerges from my marble block of words a smoothed
   form from within the wood
Arriving at the nobis of my poem, the linoleum now silent hav-
   ing sung its song.

PROLOGUE

Intimations

Could I see you, Dear Royal Household, in the Prado ever
    again?
Transformed by his then my reflections, a hall of mirrors in two
    modes:
Now in my newly-framed quality reproduction before me on my
    kitchen wall
Starting there above the top edge of my super-Mac monster
    monitor
On which I'm drafting this ninth and maybe last REFLEC-
    TION.

From Don Diego's mind and hand and palette to stretched
    canvas,
From him to me and back to him and you, through screen then
    paper, black on white
His colourings his subtle brush-strokes lost in my translations.
My translations true enough I hope, at least to some of his
    intentions,
As now I feel I am moving, still with the household, to another
    place:

You, Infanta, died in your twenties: Likewise you, the lovely
    Isabel.
You, Don Diego and the King did not then have so much longer
    to live.
So you, Nicolasito may well have beaten us all – you lived to 75!
I am now 73 and find my gaze drawn now again to Juan Nieto
Inviting us to a brightness out of and beyond this dark, high-
    ceilinged room...

From The Las Meninas Suite, "Reflection # 9".

Swansong?

So now I've named you all, my family dead and living, who mat-
   tered and still matter.
Honoured my dead, I hope by giving you meaning in my life in
   who I was and am.
Touched the living perhaps as you have touched and still are
   touching me, our changing.
Patterns emerging, disappearing, sounds with echoes, echoes
   that are sounds.

"Singing the final verse" is a Swedish line that sounds and ech-
   oes in me more and more
Especially I suppose after all those ins and outs with ambulanc-
   es, A&E, my operation:
A one month shaky transit surely from last year to this one, no
   certainties nor promises.
Okay, okay: "The final verse" this might well may be: Still sing-
   ing anyway as now.

From Family Matters, "Epilogue".

16

Getting there

Much more behind me than in front.

I've felt like that since I was 50 I suppose,
Though more, much more so now.

Nuanced by that month in hospital and a challenging operation.

My past all done and dusted, my there and then and known,
Not dead and gone though:

Memories and resonances, here now next.
The there and then of now and later:
So: who I have been, am and may still become.

The "whats" of my future all still unknown
Except for my death, of course.
Not in and of itself: the fact of it, I mean.
Mortality in practice, death confirming life.

And that I've dealt with elsewhere, anyway,
Published and unpublished.

Best left aside I suppose until it happens,
And then me quoted by a friend, or may be relative,
After the fact at my funeral.

So now too soon, too soon though closer now than ever.

And shite! I was already there as a teenage scribbler:

"when my death that must come, comes
and my dust (or mud if it's raining,) lies crushed, my body
rotten,
I wonder will I then (when?) be forgotten,
or remembered as of such a sort
best buried with his poems".

Jaysus, wrote my own epitaph at 16/17.

Ah sure, there you go, saw it coming already then.

So thank you Juliette Greco, and Sartre and Beckett, de Beau-
voir and Camus:

Kierkegaard came later and has never left me, more living than
dying.

And here it almost is again. Well, almost and almost,
Though still not quite – I mean I'm typing these lines and
Saving them later for tomorrow, I suppose.....we'll see.

So down perhaps and not yet out, waving not drowning,
To coin a phrase, half-steal one maybe, anyway borrow it...

And I can wait until my time comes, unlike Sylvia,
Not that I want or wait for it expectantly.
Or choose to beat life to it, get there first...

To coin, or steal or borrow another phrase:
My life and I: we'll do it our way!

From Family Matters, "Getting there".

PART 1

Nightcap dream

My nightcap dream of going home to die.

Diluted by reality now, has lost its taste and flavour even:
Or could be me that's lost my taste, my sense of flavour
With coughing fits after a half-decent swallow of Crested Ten
Knocked back with a younger carefree vigour an
Old man's out-of-tune optimism, hope springing eternal and all
    that...

So now it'll be my ashes flown home in a plastic urn, or posted
    or even
DHL-ed: so anyway I'm gone I'm gone of course a Monty Py-
    thon parrot, so
Now my nightcap dream is of a body burnt to ashes, a me-not-
    me, a used to be
Me gone home to be scattered in the wind off the Irish sea as it
    blusters around
The Dublin Mountains wherever who happens to be there
    might sometime like to visit.

Finally my name carved into the bottom left hand corner of the
    family headstone:
The Hanveys, Annie and Joe, Sadie, my namesake Seán, Lily,
    Maura me Ma, Kathleen, Una
And a space left to the right of me for Joanie Pony – if she
    doesn't beat me to it, of course.
And anyway, maybe as a Hanvey she'll be to the left with me
    beside her to the right and
It'll hardly matter to either of us then anyway two names on a
    headstone in Glasnevin.

Dream on

My nightcap dream of going home to die...

Though with my wheely-walker flown in with me from Sweden
Likewise my walking stick, my Swedish pensions in kronor and
My various prescriptions in English for COPD and Diabetes 2,
My chronic Lyme disease an untreatable ghost, a background
    spectre...

An old man's out-of-tune optimism, hope springing eternal and
    all that, and now
So little like it used to be, last decade, last year, last week and
    even yesterday
And I less and less who I used to be, last decade last week and
    even yesterday
Yet still here and me to myself and others, still who I was and
    am still me though

Yes and no. Yes and no. As the ma once told me , one Christmas
    I was home,
You with a glass of Dimple Haig, me with a glass of Jemmie: "it's
    awful, Seán, this getting
Old...I can see how the fall in the curtains is sagging. It's annoy-
    ing me just looking at it
And I can't stop seeing it every morning I walk into the living
    room, and then all day."

"And every now and then I find myself going to the cubbyhole
    to take out the steps and
Climb up there to adjust them – and realise I can't. No way, my
    legs, my balance, no way.
My mind plans things this oul body just can't do anymore. And
    worst is I then remember
When I could, and did." So you resigned yourself to cups of
    coffee, cigs and patience.

And it wasn't your balance you'd lost when Eilish came and
    found you dead on the floor,
A lukewarm coffee on the table, a burning ciggie in the ashtray,
    a hand of patience laid
Awaiting your turn: your heart had stopped, you'd died, so you
    and not you fell, the chair
Now marking your presence and your absence, the coffee un-
    drunk, the cig now ash the

Patience still on pause.

Still here

Awake......

Again.

Awake again:
The mild surprise of it.
And also...so fucking banal:

Did not go gentle or otherwise into that goodnight last night
    anyway...again,
And had I – not here now to know or write about it: and I am it
    seems, so there y'are.

In anyway, I'm lying here warm and dozing, knowing soon a pee
    will get me out of bed,
Maybe even get me out and up to spend another COPD/diabe-
    tes 2 – day:

Keep warm as Autumn cools the days,
Cut back on the booze, three square meals, nibbles and an
    evening snack,
Twice a day Metformin and my punctured finger-tips.

The excitement is killing me, in a manner of speaking...

Grateful for my scrabble partners and an always emerging
    poem.
(Can't resist it, sorry: scrabbling or scribbling, that's now my
    lot).

So yes, grateful for the always emerging poem.

And my personal writing more energised now in and for me
　　than the past professional.
Emerging like this one as a word, then two: attractors each and
　　both of latent themes
Each theme meeting in a node of meaning, the nodes support-
　　ing a web of themes
Expressed in words and images and allusions and the images in
　　words just as
Allusion is both word and image, itself and other simultaneous-
　　ly.

And my themes moving, shifting, I notice: not long ago, mortal-
　　ity... and now
Ageing disgracefully, to borrow a phrase from Colin Cotterill:
　　the keeping warm,
The coughing fits, peeing myself in public: the passport queue
　　at Dublin airport with a
Two-hour aircoach trip to Belfast ahead of me and no change of
　　trousers in my bags or
The opera in the new Marinsky in St. Petersburg, almost made
　　it to the loo, but not quite.

So: undignified and uncomfortable. And wet for me and smelly
　　for others I'm sure,
The sodden underpants and clinging trousers making my pres-
　　ence felt along my way...
Another way of being-in-the-world, more embodied than cog-
　　nitive I suppose:
I smell therefore I am...I am therefore I pee myself and smell
　　and in for a penny etc:
Shit myself as well, most recently in a restaurant: almost made
　　it, almost, to the loo.

Stuffed my shitty briefs deep into the waste-paper basket, paper
    towels as underwear
Getting home, uncomfortable but dry and smell-free. I'm dry
    and smell-free therefore
I am, though still ageing disgracefully it seems – must check the
    side-effects of
Metformin: ah yes, the runs. Shit! In a manner of speaking...so
The runs both front and back I suppose, both front and back...

Not to forget the less dramatic aspects of my ageing and my
    ailments:
The wheely walking frame, the armchair toilet seat, the plastic
    plank across my bath for
Sit down showering, the raised bed for my convenience getting
    into and out of it the
Sock putter on, the inhalers – yes, all the daily, hourly reminders
    of my downhill journey
To my destination, death – which it's been said "has no domin-
    ion", though believe me,

This downhill journey surely does: each day remembering yes-
    terday's catastrophes and
Each passport queue a reminder of the puddle of pee round my
    shoes in Dublin airport,
Soaked briefs and clinging trousers all the coach journey up to
    Belfast and my taxi then
To my hotel – checked in damp and smelling, though regular
    friendly guest that I am
Not a nostril twitched nor eyebrow raised, not even as I head
    for Macklin's bar for my

Traditional arrival pint, my ageing mind frantic with the logistics of new trousers...

Dry these overnight on my storage heaters, fresh underwear, breakfast, a taxi to M & S,

So, better eat now also while I'm in the bar, then head to my room, the radiators a

Shower and straight to bed. I'm thinking therefore I will be... drier and less smelly.

Unless, of course, I manage a repeat performance, or two...yes, ageing disgracefully...

Le tour

Watching the Tour de France in a scorchingly hot July both here
in Sweden and

There in France and Spain – with Thomas making a name for
himself, Sagan being

Simply, excitingly Sagan, Martin's brave breakaways with echoes
of Roche and Kelly –

My attention is drawn also to the scorched green white-mottled
hillsides,

Background becoming foreground, echoes emerging as a gener-
ating sound.

And not just green and white: the craggy rock-faced cliffs in
black-and-white:

Snow that had drifted during winter there into cracks and crev-
ices and sunken hollows

There still, preserved in shadow, the ambient warmth no match
for the focused sunshine

At changing the snow to water once again, so there and now
this process still ongoing

The frozen rain water frozen still...still, frozen, neither snow
nor ice nor water yet again.

Yet there still, still there, those scattered disconnected drifts,
the wholeness dissipated:
Neither something nor nothing, hints of the one and bits of the
other and suddenly
The mirror I have metaphored reveals itself and I am seeing
me, an identical twin
Surprised by a stranger, me yet not me, or not who I thought I
was, anyway, so more me
Maybe than an empty mirror image to be filled by my lived life,
who I was and have been

Maybe even meeting who I have become the I and me of me,
now today, who I now am
And all that formed me echoing still, still echoing, and echo
becoming sound to echo on
In and through me, the interplay of sound and echo, and sound,
the patterns of my life,
Resonances backwards and then forwards, there and then and
here-now-next, being and
Becoming me and being me all together all at once, maybe dif-
ferentiating now at last in

Facts of my life becoming metaphors of me, echoing from Euro-
sport and the Tour,
Resonating through me sound and echo and echo as sound,
meeting, merging a
Bittersweet harmony sounding around and through me: I always
preferred, it seems
The undemanding ambient warmth to any form of focused
heat, friendship rather than
Love, hugs rather than passion, receiving rather than giving,
taking rather than sharing.

Faces, names and okay, bodies drifting in and out of my anyway
now failing, even fading,
Memories with scents and smells and tastes, my mind, my nose,
my lips, my tongue, my
Hands and fingers and...a now pensioned penis – far too early
retirement, if you ask me,
But then I'm prejudiced: tried Viagra for a final fling until the
side effects and my other
Medication called a halt to that diversion from the downward
spiral of my ageing path.

And notice how that old distraction spreads its legs. The only
times that sex and love
Joined, held hands and hearts, and almost, almost shared, I
chose instead the ambient
Warmth of others' admiration – the directed sunshine of a
woman's love I first deflected
Then ignored and sidled out of into shadow, my shivering not
felt, or disregarded:
A minor irritation I could live with while I awaited its natural
disappearance, as before.

A rolling iceball now gathering momentum, growing outwards
from its frozen core
Attracting the crunchy, unfreezing drifts, responding now to the
heat of friction to
Warm it from the inside, and the warmth I feel from caring,
loving friends to turn my ice
To water once again – no longer clean and clear though flowing
maybe one last time here
As the world around me shows me who I have been and am,
different yet still me...

32

PART 2

From russia with blood

My night-time stumble in St. Petersburg heading to the loo left
    me with a sprained
Wrist, a black and blood-filled eye, and various scratches, aches
    and pains and then
The next day, peeing blood - so emergency admittance to a clin-
    ic (friend of a friend):
Ultra sounds and MRIs, and blood and urine samples every day
    and "stop the bleeding,
Get you back to Stockholm and a hospital there" and they did.
    Oh and I almost forgot

"Prostate enlargement"...doesn't rain but it pours, huh! So back
    to Stockholm and a
Urologist – if you're a man you'll know what I mean. So anyway,
    in a fortnight, surgery:
Lump in the roof of my bladder. Internal bleeding apparently
    takes precedence over
Prostate enlargement...so that's been put on hold. Just like my
    living, and I suppose my
Life now that I as a body am breaking down, short-term repair
    jobs the order of the day.

Not dying I hope not in a Swedish hospital bed, my sisters may-
be and my son kind of
Present as I go – no, no, at home in my apartment with G&Ts
and Green Spots
Celebrating our memories of each other and my leaving, in our
final family closeness,
Not that I'll be around to remember it, enjoy the Christmas
visit to the family grave: now
One of the dead there as my sister Ger belts out a Christmas
carol and berates us on the

Headstone for not fixing the Euromillions for her this year
either, our auntie Joan
Sniffles if she's there live and not with the rest of us on the
headstone and MarsBars says
Everything is "grand", so it's business as usual at the Hanvey/
Gaffney Glasnevin grave.
And Ger has bought the adjoining plot, the plain white head-
stone already in place, so
MarsBars maybe will join her, the three of us as always almost
and not quite together.

And maybe I'm jumping the gun – more in exasperation than
anticipation, frustration at
Being where I've been and am, not dying, just ageing – not
clinging to life but respecting
My organismic instinct for survival, and I admit, enjoying the
spontaneous stanza to
Stanza emergence of this my latest suite which cannot truly end
until I have done so or
End as abruptly maybe as my mother died, my ended and unfin-
ished suite...

Pre-op thoughts 1

My auntie Anne died under a general anaesthetic.
Just like I'll be under next Friday.
And Annie Goat was younger and far healthier than I am now.

She went from being a breathing person to a cooling corpse in
    one final exhalation.
Never knew what had hit her: neither then nor after.

That's what dying does to you: oblivion.

Though the body knew I'm sure.

I'm sure the the body knew its being was ending, strangely,
    prematurely even:
Matter over mind.

Mind still trying to figure it all out, the causality and sequence
    the
Explanation I suppose.
Is cognition the last to give up the ghost?

And is itself the ghost in the machine, in a manner of speaking,
    that
Haunting, taunting ever-present judge and jury, interpreter and
Know-all jester with its intimations of mortality, its embodied
    fatalism, its
Till death us do part commitment, honoured by both parties:

Becoming finally one and the same at the very end, dying to
    meet I suppose as they do
Precisely that – and both of them used to be me,
A mindless corpse now, autopsy next the
Explanation that the living bodies require for their peace of
    mind, or something...and

Fuck me, getting ahead of myself there:
From my aunt's to my own final oblivion in a few random stan-
    zas.

Wishful thinking? I hope not:
I hope to be around until there is no longer any me, a
Memory of he and him, an it to be disposed of, my matter soon
    ashes my
Mind there still in my books, in the memories of my family and
    friends, my students
Here and there, and
Me now nowhere to be seen, a
Was, a used-to-be.

Pre-op thoughts 2

Hard to practice being a
Was, a used to be.

The closest I suppose is sleeping though not really:
Unconscious if not dreaming, and the body still aware –
I can wake up with blankets on the floor, or pulled up under my
    chin my
Arms under the covers for warmth.

Dying is such a once-in-a-lifetime happening.
And in my pride I'd really like to get it right:
Succeeded mostly at anything I've dared to try or
Turned my failure into fertiliser for another seed to sow.

Always good at finding alternatives and
Running out of choices now except
To take life as it comes and then to
Die not knowing that it's happened to me.

In hospital

(1) Before

Arrived, admitted and, dressed in my operation outfit
Resting empty-headed in a bed.
Nurse Elin tells me I'm third in the queue, and then
That the surgery before me went faster than expected:
Oh great?
Oh shit?
Then me.
Bed rolled into a small and crowded theatre,
Transferred efficiently to a bed with stirrups for my legs, every-
    body doing something
Mostly to me, a focused busy-ness on my soon insensate body
    the
I of my body fading, fading

(2) During

(3) After

Came to with a new identity: 65.9.1,
Ward 65, room 9, bed 1.
Remembered only what I've said before then
Dozed and slept.

Drank loads of water to flush the blood out of my bladder.

Had cream of chicken with potato gratin for my first food of
    the day, then
Dozed and slept then
Haven't done it since I was a baby I suppose – shit the bed I
    mean.
An adult now I waddled bowlegged to the bathroom and shit
    the toilet bowl, and seat
And lid and floor and walls and me and all the while Nurse
    Niklas made my bed, then
Joined me in my various travails – the catheter dangling from
    my willy with tubes down
My thigh to the piss-bag strapped to my left thigh held in a
    stocking on my left calf – all
In the way of my sitting on the shitty loo, letting my gut and
    arsehole do their things,
Which they anyway did regardless as guts and arseholes do then
    Niklas
Hosed me down, front and back, my body bits my catheter and
    tubes and bloody bag and
The little left of my imagined dignity, my ageing disgracefully
    totally confirmed.

So dried and dressed in a change of hospital clothing, and,
    helped by Niklas into bed I'm
Sitting up and drinking water, reflecting on my day and my pre-
    vious reflections, my life
Then and now, and theirs, Nurse Niklas and earlier Nurse Mia
    who checked my catheter,
My pee-bag and approved so
What the fuck's my problem?
Who the fuck do I think I am?

Here, I'm a body to be done to, tended and sent home, no
    longer a professor, therapist,
Trainer, author, know-all – a body merely, a medical object nei-
    ther graceful nor
Disgraceful except in my own eyes jaundiced by all of who I
    used to be, my standing in
Society and all that other shit I gave attention to until today
    when my own diarrohea
Painted me, my bedclothes, the loo, the bathroom, my personal
    plumbing that watery
Brownish yellow, yellowish brown that is the palette of shitting
    myself – again!

Remembered suddenly the ma's kinda sorta resignation to her
    new reality, her life
Condensed to coffee, a fag, a hand of patience, her neighbour
    Eilish and a visit from her
Children, mine once a year at Christmas...sorry ma, sorry: I
    know your isolation now the
Loneliness of ageing, the relentless disintegration of a body still
    alive, and a mind

Recording it for any one who'll listen: so ageing, simply ageing –
     and so a minor triumph:
Last night my first pee since my homecoming without blood, so
     healing as I age and
Ageing, simply ageing...

PART 3

May 9, 2019

Today you are would have been 47, though for me...still
Still and forever 14, well
14 years and three months to the day a
Sharp breath, shocked stare and gone.

Dead and gone.

Forever.

Forever dead and gone.

Though also also
Always always in and with me as long as I live, and... your moth-
    er, probably, and your
Auntie Ger – there with us in the house in Dublin when you
    were born...

Your big brother in your Granny Maura's, so
Ger, me, the mobile midwives, your mother, your
Death assailed her, left her someone else somewhere else,
There (where?) still it seems and you there with her I'm sure, as
    you are with me now
On your would-have-been day as you will be with me again in
    three months to the day,
Birth day death day, your days, our days and
All those in-between days, in Dublin first then Stockholm
    where you died.

Sharp breath, shocked stare and gone.

Gone too our family quartet a violent
Amputation back to our early trio though unrecognised, not
    really
Anymore an "us", an awkward and reluctant used to be, an
Out-of-practice trio going self-consciously through the motions
    of a dead quartet a
Dead and gone quartet and then a
Dead marriage confirming an already dead relationship.

And all those in-between days, those 33 years of your would-
    have-been-days a
Poem for you each birthday emerging as this one in all the
    grieving for your absence
Yet again your absence, and my memories of you – and not only
    the shocked stare the
Homework battles we had, the "stolen" bicycles, the Sunday
    walks to the pool,
You, me and your brother while your mother slept off her nurs-
    ing night-shift and

Now for the first time in a long, long time our
Family quartet together and named again on
This, your would have been day.

Over my shoulder and under my nose

After all the angst, the fear and trembling the
Flooding back and front the
Further tests and checks and meetings a
Prostate resection procedure with a
Three month waiting list, well
What can I say?
Or do?

Slow down, take stock...

Nostalgia maybe?
Maybe nostalgia...

Much more behind me than in front and my
Now a dreary, daily repetition of
Pills, punctured tips, dashing to the loo, diapers, eating drinking
    sleeping waking my
Writing all I have to look forward to each day apart from
Visiting friends both here and there so
With you here and now in time and space our
Mutual visiting here on the screen or page...

Nostalgia then, though
Nuanced by regret and
Not for anything said or done or happened more
Not said nor done, the roads not taken the
Might-have-beens that never were nor
Ever will be so not even a road less travelled one
Glimpsed and then
Avoided?
Evaded? Anyway

Not chosen so not taken not experienced an
Absence like the gap between my lines and stanzas a
Necessary and defining presence also, not there and yet
Directing the flow of time and space and me
Defining who I was have been and am
Gaps and all: so was was not, have been not been yet am with
All the might have beens of me both there and somehow here
Here somehow in my regrets of them my roads not taken and
     all with
Names of people and places I notice as they resonate in my
     mind and
Most of the people women and
Women in bright places often where the woman was the
Sunshine and the light, heat aimed at or offered me and I
Running or slinking off to bask in the warm safety of admiration
     yes
Swedes and maybe others will remember now as I do
Doctor Glas: Loved, Admired, Feared, Hated and Held in con-
     tempt.
His alternative ways of being in the world grabbed me once and
     never let me go so
In the absence of loved, admired – a flash and shock as I evoke
Two photos and two women and in each the woman
Gazing warmly at me from the side while I
Smile my reluctant smile straight at the camera my reluctance
     to be
Caught as two when I was always one, me alone or me
Distinctive in a crowd and so of course alone there also.

So there you have me and here I am and
Now revealed my saddest regret: too late for love my
Snowman camouflage now become me.

Full circle

Back at my local clinic I sat by Sister Hanna's desk and we
   discussed
Leakages of the bladder and the bowels as nonchalantly as if we
   were
Chatting distractedly about world politics and then got down to
   business:
Choosing protective products for me as a pensioner who had
   pissed and shit himself.

Triangles of absorbent padding to catch my pre-pee mini flow
   and post-pee drops and
Then a padded strip to cover my openings front and back
   should be adequate if I am
Reducing my intake of Metformin so fewer caught short shits.
   We agree that this feels
Better for me than the brief-shaped diapers also on offer, more
   acceptable anyway, yes!

Ah! So that's what this is – back to the beginning my past my
   present and it seems my
Future as long as I happen to live. Tough shit in a manner of
   speaking not liquid so a
Step in the right direction I suppose. And still have my own
   teeth so could be worse just
Get my feet sorted and a supply of inhalers and me and my
   walker are ready to roll...

Angels playing with my heart
(For Eugenio and Phil)

A good friend asked me recently if I expected to meet Dara
  when I died and
Programmed Irish Catholic that I was and kind of am still and
  wishful thinker also I
Quietly whispered yes and then reflected: something I'd taken
  for granted a challenge
Now a put up or shut up moment: so do I or don't I expect to
  meet Dara when I die and

Then the following day an American friend mailed me to say
  that he expected to get to
Heaven before me – prostate cancer with all the treatment
  options for his consideration
And decision the sooner the better so worse off healthwise than
  I am now, anyway now
And with a buddy in Jesus his treatment will be bearable his
  heavenly place assured and

Having already dealt with my death it's now the turn of my
  afterlife it seems so
Let me begin at the beginning with Dara's death and funeral
  and public mass where
Pater Hornung improvised a sermon to include Dara's school-
  pals who were present his
Theme "The meaning of life for a boy who dies at 14" – seems
  like such a waste he said

Though only mainly if we think in terms of achievement, success, reputation and public

Legacy maybe of some sort so he proposed an alternative more personal much more

Subjective, owned by each of us in our own way our own unique memory of Dara and

How knowing him has changed us, added a dimension to who we are simply by his

Coming into our lives and gave himself as an example, a German Jesuit missionary in a

Country of Lutherans and free-church evangelicals and other religions and none who

Never met Dara yet stood by his coffin as he led the funeral service and now leads a

Memorial service and preaches a sermon in a church almost as full of strange faces as

His first mass here after he had just arrived as a new priest at Saint Eugenia's – what a

Gift from Dara! "And that's the meaning of Dara's life to me, today and until the day I die"

That thanks to Dara coming into his life, he, a Catholic missionary now found himself

Giving an impromptu sermon to a church with more non-parishoners than ever before.

Later, Pater Hornung became my father confessor, a gift for both of us from Dara and I

Trained to be a psychotherapist, a kind of priest and confessor, the ripples spreading....

Then every year I felt his presence with me on his birthday,
    then his death day each time
Celebrating his presence with a poem. And also with me in plac-
    es we had been and even
Places we had never been I thought he'd like. And he is always
    13-14. Never older than
That day he died though I'd moved on from 44 and now to 76
    with failing health though
Here still hanging on in here and that tamed and shrunken part
    of me that's rational and
Pragmatic can't help wondering how old we each would be were
    we to meet where and
Whenever it is that we might meet when both of us are dead
    and not just him and I with
Him in mind, always and forever 14

So okay: not me as I am now nor you as you were then not each
    of us before we died the
Bodies burned so ashes to dust. And I need to be alive to bring
    you to mind so when I die
You in my mind dies also and out of mind out of sight and
    memory and hope or even
Wishful thinking – is that where I see us meeting? My American
    friend is surely sure that

Jesus will be there for him with open arms – my wishful think-
    ing is no match for such a
Certainty grounded in faith while I believe when it suits me I
    suppose like when asked if
I expected to meet you when I died I whispered yes old habit
    and my wishful thinking
Camouflaging my emptiness and doubts supporting my illusions
    a brave face on my

Cowardly evasion and those days maybe coming to an end now
    that I'm nearing not only
My own end but also finding meaning in that well-intentioned,
    insightful question and
Reflecting deeply on my answer rooting around in the cellars of
    my being opening doors
To dusty rooms I thought were closed and opening their win-
    dows to let in air and light.

Meetings

Clearly you're still with me Dara though always in my mind and
    in my
Memories of you made perhaps more vivid by your death and so
Keeping you alive in me and acknowledging also that you're
    dead your body
Burned to ash and strewn by me on a hillock in a Solna, Sweden
    cemetery, so
Gone from here but not forgotten no no not forgotten so here
    in me as I am although not
Here as you are but as you were and as a corpse of course there
    in your hospital bed and
Later when your brother was rushed home from Dublin on a
    trolley in the chapel the
Very last I saw though not of you my son though recognisably
    your "remains" as they're
So rightly known already rotting from the inside as the poisons
    of your treatment
Bubbled from your nose leukaemia and its treatment bubbling
    from your cooling
Remains and I happy I had said "no" to an autopsy which could
    have meant your
"Fresh" remains being scalpelled in a morgue before your broth-
    er made it back to
Meet you dead and gone and his mother and father and yours
    there with you both a
Final final time our family square a strange triangle now lopsid-
    ed somehow and soon
Not even that a trio becoming a pair and a single though still a
    family triangle anyway in

Theory for a while, and then another death of sorts, the father
    son now family as
Mother and wife elsewhere in time and space and her father
    died she further away and
Look! The four of us together yet again even if only on this page
    and Dara yes is anyway
Still dead and gone and so a triangle of sorts rather than a resur-
    rected square another
Remains I suppose though not to be seen...

So do I expect to see and meet you when I die and both of us
    have gone from living to
Remains to ovens and to ash and then? My evangelical friend
    liked a phrase I used "the
Certainty of faith" – not fact or reason or science: faith: what he
    has and I have maybe
Lost along my way or as I wrote to Pater Dominik, current suc-
    cessor as Parish priest to
Dear Pater Hornung I am maybe more a lost than a prodigal
    son. We'll see...

Crossings

I celebrated your birthday on May 9 at would have been 47 and
    now I'm
Moving towards your deathday August 9 when you will be and
    are 33 years dead, this
No-day vacuum of your absence your special presence in and of
    my life between your
Birth and death a three-month metaphor of your 14 years of
    living and my 76 so far

Keeping you alive in me though always and still unsure of you
    alive in you somehow
Alive in you as you or anyway a you I'd recognise embodied as
    you were for me as you as
DarsBars, Darsy, Dara the Bara or Dara! when you were stroppy
    and/or me impatient or
Under orders, you the object of the two of us our battles old
    and new and then you died

Sharp breath shocked stare and gone. Family and marriage died
    with you, marriage and
Relationship died with you and I to my shame at times lived on
    my lifeline keeping you
Alive within me while much of that around me though not your
    brother dead or lost its
Meaning and I hanging on in there for dear life a passive living
    body in a dead sea of the

Corpse of my personhood floating aimlessly from coast to coast
blown by whatever wind
Life happened to blow until it blew me back to therapy this
time a group where I
Felt fully at home so fully that you could be there with me dead
as body and alive in me a
Spirit experienced though not seen outside of my memory and
imagination anyway real

Real for me in those instants of your presence in and with me
and outside of me as I am
Now before my death and burning body to ashes to ashes to
dust and dust to dust our
Spirits maybe or whatever meeting wherever they then may be.
Yeah, I can buy that our
Okay then our disembodied souls meeting so still not us as we
have been father and son

Daddy and DarsBars Darsy Dara the Bara Christ how I've
missed you who you were then
Were then and were becoming so missed and missed out on you
our time together then
Now and next warped by your death and my witnessing of you
in that instant fixing us in
Time and space though death ends time and changes space
surely as I know them so a

Time and space in and of an other time and space than here and
    now and when I'm dead
Dead in this time and space and gone elsewhere no longer me as
    who I was nor here as
Here is for me now elsewhere in an other space who knows
    anyway not me though
Probably my angels who I'm sure will each of them smile when
    they receive and read

These my closing lines I feel of this my maybe final suite who
    knows anyway not I now
Faced with believing I can transform my wandering and my
    wishful thinking into well
Well faith I suppose and a community I never really had the
    guts or conviction to ever
Really leave those masses in Milano, Riga Tallinn and Stock-
    holm of course. And Liza with

Her Russian Orthodox icons of Celtic saints pre-schism, her
    books and my namesake
Gordey Seán his christening in St. Petersburg, Orthodox
    Church of The Annunciation the
Road not always straight the map not always followed though
    here I am it seems back at
The door and knocking: what I thought was a one-way journey
    now shown to be return?

Dara again 2019
May 9 1972 – August 9 1986

Lying in bed this morning in the cozy no-man's land between
    sleeping and dozing and

Dozing and getting up my thoughts turn to this morning all
    those years ago when you I

Now know would awaken to later cross the every man's frontier
    of death and I who'd

Watched you dying shared your room still hoping that last week
    of your life would

Soon enough now see you die sharp breath shocked stare across
    that last frontier to an

Other place and timelessness where I would not be either there
    or then and still not

There or then though closer getting closer to my own crossing
    and our meeting maybe

Maybe possibly probably our meeting: that challenge of faith
    again okay okay our

Meeting in an other time and where our meeting is its own
    place heaven already now for

Me anyway just the thought of it even the guilt of all my short-
    comings as a father then

Dissipating in this my confession and your forgiveness of me as
    I can now experience the

Grace I'm opening to and welcoming and it seems receiving
    Dara in this my living

Conversation with you on your death-day also as other memo-
    ries are evoked and find

Meaning in the wholeness of who we were and are though liter-
    ally worlds apart now

Here and elsewhere simultaneously here apart and elsewhere as
in this poem together a

Togetherness unique to us just now and which I celebrate by
sharing here with others a

Presence surely of an angel in my life my personal guide who is
always here on your

Birth and death days and any time I need you in between to
grace me with your simply

Being where you are yet here within me also and I see you as a
memory or wish and

Glad now looking back I didn't know that the Northern Cemetery spread out beneath the

Children's Cancer ward floor nine of Karolinska held the chapel
where Pater Hornung

Gently and firmly would lead your funeral service and where I'd
stop for a prayer on my

Way with your plastic urn to the hill beyond the chapel to the
left there topped by the

Memorial Garden where I would strew your ashes the last of
you in this world so bad

Enough your dying and your death without imagining that aftermath played out there

Beneath and beyond your window bad enough your dying and
your death there and

Then now here in my retelling of what I saw and you my son
went through and a vague

Awareness as I recount these memories and reflections of a
shift of sorts form and focus

Shifting shifting to resettle and rest as if time and place had
shifted in and for me and us..

Anam cara

Finally, finally I understand it (I think), this magical Celtic
   phrase. I mean I
Get it, (kind of) get it not only with and in my head – my heart
   my body my soul the
Wholeness of me who I once was have been and am me as I can
   now
Experience my being as my having become and still becoming,
   moving and still, still
Emerging a moth attracted by a flame vaguely remembered
   ignored and then almost
Almost overlooked now flickering again maybe finally sensing
   what I'd thought I'd seen
Understanding what I'd thought I'd known though now and
   here and therefore new and
I becoming other than before and elsewhere also so not a return
   a new beginning a
Choice this time a decision guided supported affirmed by others
   so no longer either
Alone or even on my own: I'd met some people on my journey
   who somehow maybe
Knew and shared my destination could and did help me on my
   way each of you my
Anam cara then, my soul's friend no no not not my "soul mate"
   no no way a wholly
Wholly other relationship a spiritual intimacy emerging from
   closeness as friends and
Travelling companions on shared or parallel journeys anyway
   connected, touching
Touching each other in our various ways anyway each of you
   touching me deeply as I

Greet air and light into my dusty cellar's corridors and rooms
and I acknowledge now

Facets anyway of who I am becoming have become: A Practising
Catholic of sorts a

Grateful pilgrim on life's camino with other pilgrims there and
here and always here my

Anam cara and my choir of angels if ever I meet you all together,
who knows.......

PART 4

In No Man's land

How strange it is how strange this being
Here not there there where I have and would have been at
those
Conferences and gatherings collegial meals and evening tête a
têtes not
Now nor ever again there nor here much longer anyway and
Already dead for some I sense as e-mails criss-crossed cyber
space and
Filled my screen with greetings for each other and those
Well-laid plans for meetings and then
Counting off the seatings and the
Limitations of my age and ailments anyway somewhat known it
seems I'm
Gently not included and this my after death experience before
my actual
Death's oblivion and obliviousness the vacuum of our parting
Now already already now in this my no man's land.

Travel documents

Odd that I've seen my boarding pass my sister found that day
the ma

Lost her patience on the table there with her coffee and her
ashtray as her heart

Stopped dead and her body fell off her chair and onto the liv-
ing-room floor a

Contradiction she would have "twigged" as she used to say
knowingly so yes my

Boarding pass dated and timed and typed and carboned no not
printed typed and

Carbon-copied there in The Rotunda Maternity Hospital Dub-
lin in August 1942 or

19420822 as the Swedes would have it where I've lived for more
than half my

Journey to Departures while first the Ma and then th'oulfella
then Dara my son and

Cathy my partner came and went in a manner of speaking and I
was with them both

Dara and Cathy as their spirits became ghosts and then as their
bodies burned and I

Emptied their ashes in places I could visit and now maybe on
my way again to visit

Another them who knows not I though could be they know and
have already met

There wherever that is that they maybe are together they who
never met in life so

Them and not them as I as who I then was then knew them as
who they were then and I

Here now as I have become my ticket and boarding pass all
registered and valid including

72

Lounge access it seems my passport known the visa automatic I
   suppose at birth affirming
My yes my mortality my death proof that I have lived the I and
   me of who I was a memory
Others may have of who I have been was alive for them though
   I am dead and gone

Getting here

I first sensed the end was nighing I suppose that second time in
    Belfast with

Pneumonia again third winter in a row Belfast St.Petersburg
    Belfast and that

Kinda sorta insult for a Southern Republican being covered by
    the NHS born

As I was a Brit still in the Commonwealth before we became a
    Republic so

Treatment and full board for my 8-day stay including all my
    tests the verdict

COPD to join the Lyme Disease I'd had for years too late to
    treat that shadow

Ever-present in my veins and then fainting/falling falling/faint-
    ing in and out of

A&E and the Neuro wards with maybe epilepsy maybe heart or
    stroke or yes a

Blocked carotid so a five hour operation then later more check-
    ups and tests and

Yet another diagnosis this time Diabetes 2 (or too?) and pills
    and blood-sugar

Tests and dietary suggestions exercise and check-ups and assess-
    ments then that

Stumble in St.Petersburg and blood-red pee to pinkish pee and
    ultrasounds and

MRIs and stop the bleeding get you home and by the way your
    prostate is

Enlarged at least so have it looked at back in Stockholm so I did
    and bladder

Surgery false alarm expanding prostate pushing in the bladder
wall so put on

Waiting list for prostate reduction surgery then right hand not
knowing what

Left hand is doing called for a prostate biopsy worse much
worse than a finger

Up my arse or a camera through my willie some kind of cattle
prod with scissors

Six snips in all I think at least and then the verdict prostate
cancer so samples to

Oncologists in the hospital where I saw my youngest son Dara
die for their

Verdict and suggestions for treatment and my age and general
condition and mere

Medium risk of impending death supported a no surgery pro-
posal with maybe

Hormone treatment so back to the urologist for a treatment
plan prescription and

Assessment schedule though as he said "you're more likely to
die Seán of a heart

Attack or stroke, much faster and less painful" and I suppose
he's got a point...

Then, Now, Next 1

It used to be angels on pin-heads engaging Catholic minds and
    now it seems its
Ashes and the Resurrection when Gabriel's doing his thing and
    calling us to our
Heavenly Home well anyway those of us both called and chosen
    and in one piece
One piece it seems the central issue one so even when its ashes
    gathered as one
Cremated body in one urn one designated resting place no not
    the mantlepiece no
A designated resting place private though accessible a columbar-
    ium for example so
Forget the ashes blowing in the wind or floating on the rippling
    currents of a river
Heaving rollers of the sea or Dara's poured from the urn to one
    side of the formal
Memorial Site or Cathy's in the shelter of a rock she liked to
    rest on when we
Walked our dog around our local island just down the hill and
    over the bridge so both
Their ashes open to wind and rain and ice and snow and well
    dissipation so the
Congregation of the Faith in Rome would not approve but
    then again neither of them
Practising Catholics Cathy probably baptised and christened in
    a Catholic church by her
Irish Catholic parents and Dara well the tried and trusted baby
    bath method granny and

Aunties taking turns no doubt to be sure to be sure and proba-
  bly his mother in the
Sun-trap yard having a smoke and glad of the help bathing the
  babby as they said so
Have I scuppered their chances on Judgement Day and what of
  my own must check or
Maybe trust that faith and religion don't always need to match
  like when I took communion
Not bothering with confession communion as expression of my
  faith confession a question of
Rules of the Church and then I learned that the only sins block-
  ing communion would be
Murder including abortion according to the rules so okay any-
  way even by the rules faith
Rules okay and not convenience maybe this time if at all but
  more conviction heart and
Soul of course heart and soul and do the coffins rise up whole
  again as the body's ashes
Embody again for the final journey so heart and soul together
  again in flesh and blood the
Whole of us as one again though spirit soon its earthly journey
  done and well...dusted the
Spirit timeless now so back to the future I suppose in our old
  earthly terms so yes faith rules.

Reminiscenses 1
Spain

Armchair cyclist that I am of course I watched the Vuelta just
    as I had the

Giro and the Tour and now the climax of this final circuit of the
    season the

Streets and squares and circles of Madrid the loom to hold the
    warp and weft of

Versions of the cyclists' weaving of earlier and emerging pat-
    terns so yes

Madrid Madrid of The Prado and The Prado of Velásquez and
    so of course of

Las Meninas and that dark high-ceilinged room his gallery and
    studio another

Place another there I'll visit in my mind and never be again and
    more than just

Madrid the Prado and Velásquez his Las Meninas my memories
    also of

Barcelona and Picasso´s urban palaces his 58 versions from
    Velásquez and

Most of all where Pablo opens the shutters and the sharp Span-
    ish sunlight

Illuminates the stage that Don Diego painted his players on
    from memory all

Arranged as if viewed by their king and queen and then by us
    the viewers and

Certainly by me whose versions are reflections in words and
    images on the

Players and their monologues and meetings and maybe even
    meaning in

Whole and parts of the original painting and its derivatives of
course Picasso and
Degas and Dali and Manet and mirrors and gazing subjects
watching the watchers
Watching them watching them a hall of mirrors imitating life
and life then
Imitating art it seems it seems who knows my reminiscenses a
dance in
Time and timelessness a then now next in time both real and
imagined a dance of
Dying and death at the end of life all past the future shrinking
to its coming silence.

Interludes

I

Not sure who said it so maybe the bible at either end or Shake-
    speare but anyway where
There's life there's hope and my new version that where there's
    dying there's living so
There I am at 77 flat on my back my calves in stirrups and the
    same urologist who'd
Stuck his finger up my arse and then a camera up or down my
    willie waited with his
Scalpelled cattle prod aimed at my asshole and then my prostate
    his head bobbing up
Between my thighs to urge me to would-you-believe-it "relax"
    for fuck's sake with a
Cattle prod with snippers up my arse and my right thigh held in
    the hands of a vivacious
Middle Eastern brunette and the other in the safe warm hands
    of a former Soviet coast
Smiling Baltic blonde relax he's just got to be kidding and then
    the nurses left me to his
Devices and went to package and mark my prostate bits and the
    discomfort back so you
Can take the erection out of the man but you can't take the
    man out of the erection relax?

Reminiscenses 2
Italy

First met you Caravaggio on a business trip to Parma in a
    church there maybe a basilica face-to-face from walls or also
Down from domed ceilings naves or apses or whatever I'd
    Google myself only I'd have to save and close then find this
    page
Again lost many a poem or paper that way well lost and lost just
    never found again so in my fading memory only and also
There well here still still hiding on a hard disk a new name may-
    be in my rush to save and close and move location so
Still there just like Merisi and in Parma still for me until Milano
    and the Brera and the archway there framing your
Emmaus those two apostles and the wayfaring stranger they'd
    met in their frightened flight what started as a meal a
Miracle now the risen Christ revealed the inn-folk focussed on
    their work not witnesses though clearly present at a
Lazarus moment darkness of death and burial to light of resur-
    rection and reunion the mission now up and running
Faith and death and resurrection revealed though not as yet
    questioned by Thomas nor tested by his probing finger the
Wounded body that had died with them again and living and
    soon to be what what Swedes call "Christ the Flyer" on
Ascension Thursday their secular irreverence some kind of play-
    ful echo of Thomas and his bewildered humanity that
Humanity you capture in the resurrected Christ a man amongst
    others his incarnation affirmed by his death his Godhead
With them in their startled reactions to His resurrection and
    the prophesies fulfilled their flight halted futures unknown
    and
Once when I was there I saw the tail-end of a queue I'd say
    there to the left outside a door or anyway an

Entrance of some sort so I added myself to the end of what was
in fact a queue and very slowly moving just 1 step now and
then

Then I saw the light a large high-ceilinged room walls bare an
easel in the centre destination of the queue a chair or stool

There also and could it be and oh my God or Christ it was Man-
tegna's Lamentation and what a way to show it each one of

Us our patient and respectful wait rewarded with a private view-
ing and then my turn just me and John the Marys and

Mantegna's bearded blood-drained corpse of Christ waked and
anointed ready for the shroud the stone to block and then

Open the tomb and Christ to take the path would take him to
Emmaus where you would paint a young androgynous and

Recently resurrected Christ breaking bread with two disciples
and there behind you to the left the crucified dead body a

Before and after study where the before is also an after in our
knowledge and the brutalised hands and feet a gospel story

Here in the Brera the Brera in Milano two Renaissance Italians
retelling old stories in the secular 1980's and I am then as

A chiaroscuro of shadowy tradition bright reason a basket over
the edge tension of my will I won't I topple with the scat-
tered

Still life a confusion of disconnected fruit falling rolling ran-
domly as I've become my given form in dissipation changing
and

Reforming inside out so me still me though different surely
maybe saved and not yet closed though maybe logging out as

Age and illness take their toll and I too have had my Matthew
moment called not chosen then so maybe now the second
time around

Not suddenly like Saul more your innkeeper I suppose an
onlooker who has seen the light experience lit by reflection
into

Acceptance and acceptance into quiet open faith...

Interludes

2

And in the middle of all of this I moved apartment just down a
    few floors from my
Eagle's nest top floor of a building right on the outer rim of a
    hill of rock on one side
Overlooking a Baltic inlet innermost islands of Stockholm's
    archipelago the other the
Royal park and lake and now the multifaith chapel where neigh-
    bours and friends
Cried and smiled and laughed our way through Cathy's funeral
    and to the left the local
Kindergarten and in the middle me with what I have left of life
    before it's my turn in the
Chapel or my parish church from move to removal in seven
    lines just like life the end in
Place from first breath to last rattle which in Cathy's case I
    heard your hand in mine you
Dara I couldn't touch the pain no longer a person a poisoned
    body drifting to its end and
You as Dara had already left us the day before as I recall so
    waiting for your body to join
You and it did that afternoon and more than likely my turn next
    or anyway soon another
Move of sorts so just as well I'm getting in some practice at "not
    taking it with me" nor
Leaving too much behind for my son and sisters friends to
    dump along with my remains.

PART 5

Messages

I smile as I recall then and now and how time was I'd head for
the door as the letter-box clattered and
Post slapped and skittered on the hall floor just lay there passive
and patient only a logo or an actual
Stamp whispering a possible probable source evoking a first
reaction smile frown grunt profanity or
Curiosity even even curiosity though less and less of that these
days these days it's mainly bills reminders
Threats of further action or notices of further action already as
forecast taken irreversibly taken over and
Out of my control or interest even now that my statistically
impending death edges closer with friendly
Winks and nudges from philosophical me to my ageing body
with its ailments and my history of less than
Ideal lifestyle all catching up and overtaking me it seems others'
gloomy predictions finally realised past
Present now my present old past my future more present until
it too is past with me or without me and if
Without me then what the hell or who knows heaven even in
that then and now still here a man still of
Flabby flesh and medicated blood exchanging messages with
myself sender and recipient the I and me of
Who we have become as one so whole complete and finished
these final lines and full stop so definitive we
Hesitate to let one of us so abruptly end our soft duet yet here
we go I've done it.

Doh Soh

So doh soh as they say in Sweden, meaning something like now
that all that

Could and by implication should be said and/or done has been
it anyway seems

Time to take the next logical rational step move on from where
we have been

Still are it seems or maybe were and now that we are moving
leaving there

Changing as we move moving as we change and doh soh could
and/or should be

Elsewhere now than where we were and sorry just doesn't seem
so really but

Different clearly different I mean I'm writing now again having
feared I'd lost it

Lost and found again it seems my art and craft so is it then my
theme I've lost in

Other words I've lost my way my thread my direction the there
now next of my

Existential ruminations the meaning of my where and what and
whither so even

Whether my whither is a concern apart from meeting my dead
son Dara you so

Suddenly with me these days again having recently moved I
found your photos

Today the ones where we had your hair cut to cover your moult-
ing from the

Poisons aimed at fighting the poison of your leukemia bald bony
dying but still

You so playfully fully you as I recall from our walks in your
   wheelchair how you
Doffed your cap to neighbours and passing strangers as we
   walked local streets
Those closing days of your short life fourteen years and three
   months to the day
Sharp breath shocked stare and gone gone then now and forever
   gone unless of
Course we meet elsewhere in time and space and anyway here
   with me now so
Doh soh on this your big brother's 50th birthday and in my
   hand the card the
Father's Day card I found with your photos bought no doubt by
   your mother who
Got you both to sign and give to me and even a photo of you
   both is not as real as
Your two childish signatures slopey and slightly sloppy under
   duress no doubt and
Now magical magical in my hand my eyes my heart the whole of
   me on this my
First-born's fiftieth with the photos of his dead little brother
   and their signed card
Uniting the two of you again and I again a father with two sons
   alive for me alive.

Endings

I've lived beside a Baltic inlet in Stockholm North for decades
  now with

Over the water across and above I mean the local landmark an
  actual

Folly a Scottish castle compressed into Cedergren's vertical
  tower ever

Upwards and outwards as he nourished his belief his life would
  end as his

Project ended so maybe a metaphor for me to ponder as I work
  on this my

Could be final suite and wonder how to bring it to a meaningful
  close alive

Still as I happen to be still here while life moves in and through
  me to our

Shared ending death death too of my reflections and my writing
  I mean I

Won't be here to reflect on my experience of dying nor work on
  my emerging

Words and lines to tie the sack as they say in Sweden the sack
  here being my

Aspects of Ageing Suite these closing not quite yet final steps of
  my being here

Gently anyway for now fading into the memories of others and
  my books as

Proof of my presence my footprint here in time and space soon
  enough to be

Erased in turn by time and space as my spirit eases into time-
  lessness itself

Its own space then I hope with other spaces and is my suite a
  Cedergren in

Reverse of sorts my project ending before I do: soh doh soh...

Sunsets

Natural I know and yet just can't help noticing how my tired-
    ness follows me from rising to retiring so

24/7 as I've nowadays learnt to say in other words all fucking day
    as my afternoon nap went from

Indulgent luxury to necessity to indulgent choice as nowadays
    reflecting on this afternoon in fact that

Here in my new home well new and new downsizing in the
    same building smaller cheaper and from

Floor 8 to 4 so top to middle and up there with a view a vista
    really over a Baltic inlet inner islands of the

Archipelago and I sometimes saw above the buildings the royal
    lake so water from every window the

Balcony deserving of an eagle and me with fading eyesight all
    the ailments of my ageing still with me here

Here on my new balcony its close-up view of the chapel and to
    my left the kindergarten to my right the

Reddening clouds of the setting sun strange how I never
    watched the sun set from my eyrie in the sky nor

Looked from a window as it sank beyond the lake and now I see
    it every day from my desk through the

Balcony door and glazing both kitchen windows also at day's
    end and always always the chapel that

Chapel where I organised the funeral of my lovely Cathy a cele-
    bration of our life together up there and

Here in this well-intentioned half-failed Christian project of a
    village from christening through marriage a

Baptism or so and charismatic Sunday services then funerals for
    villager after villager and then my turn a

Variation on community I suppose an echo of my own inten-
tions and attempt a chance not really taken so
Thanks now to my angels and my anam cara I got to have a
second chance or maybe third at least so if at
First I didn't succeed try try and okay fourth chance try again as
Jesus Mary and Joseph already know I'm
Awkwardly back reluctantly even exchanging my self chosen
exile with its freedom of sorts for all of the
Constraints of faith and its obligations its give and get in my
communities now of two with my Spanish
Guardian angel here in Stockholm and my Russian anam cara
how she gives across the centuries with
Orthodox icons of pre-schism Celtic saints Patrick Brigid
Brendan Columbanus and I respond and share
The Brendan Voyage with its uilleann pipes and give her name
and honour her in this my latest suite as the
Winter sun staring at me me staring back through the hollowed
cupola across on the chapel roof our
Sunset times approaching the one calculated predictable so
certainly this afternoon and mine who knows
Though coming surely surely coming and I already waning into
it not needing a skull on my desk or a
Graveyard to reflect in had those now all I need is here the
chapel and our setting suns the silence here...

Mary coming down to Earth

You were present of course at your son's conception an
Angel it's said announcing your
Impregnation by something outside of your experience a Jewish
   virgin barely
Bat Mitzvahed now suddenly
Pregnant your childhood suddenly over your menstruations
   suddenly suspended the
Confusion of it all then present also with Elizabeth your cousin
   who
Knew both pregnancy and giving birth a
Hasty betrothal maybe with a local Yusef who
Took you pregnant on a journey to appease the conqueror so off
   you set to Bethlehem a
Family almost though soon enough though soon enough so
Present very present as your son now there with you so not just a
Virgin conception also a virgin birth and surely
Suckled by you as you had seen your village neighbours suckling
   and as
Elizabeth had taught you birthing and caring for your newborn
   son now with you and
Here on earth with us and so you
Fade now into absence it seems then
Present very present in Cana with your stroppy teenage son now
   wise enough to know
Just who is who with a Jewish mother and when to let his moth-
   er do the talking and so
His time suddenly come to go about His Father's business the
   water into wine though
Thanks to you and you now feeling the first pain perhaps of
   separation of your

Motherly fears for him still yours whose time it seemed had
    come so now an

Other's also and his lonely own on a journey only He could
    make so back into

Lonely absence again as his public ministry begins then ends
    there in your

Presence again now on that hill of suffering and death and the

Evangelists replaced now as artists imagine your journey their

Pietas and paintings showing us your pain your sorrow your
    distress and

Rumour has it you may have met Him risen when He maybe
    visited James at home and

Even the stroppiest Jewish son could not do other than ac-
    knowledge his mother in the

Family home so maybe you saw him mocked and dying a dead
    and broken body then

Entombed and heard of the body gone risen it was said a mira-
    cle proclaimed and then

Him and also him now home and greeting you your

Motherhood ended your

Glory awaiting you in your assumption and now that I've met
    you here in words so

Present for and in me here and now so

Holy Mary mother of God pray for me a sinner now and at the
    hour of my death amen.

Easter

Patterns amaze me always

Emerging brightly from surrounding shadows the pattern

Of me clearly yet also there outside of me so I can

Experience it inside and out so feel its meaning only for me and

Wider relevance maybe maybe so shared if I can

Adequately describe the two perspectives so it

All began with my anam cara Liza's Eastern icon of the Annunciation and I

Shocked in current time at its closeness to the Passion, death and

Resurrection of the Child she bore gave birth to suckled surely and whose degradation and death she would

Witness whose broken body she would straighten in his tomb and if rumours are to be

Believed must have met when He her son yet not her son was risen and visited His now

Half-brother James so Mary knew conception now from a sexual perspective also the

Pregnancy and birth a been-there-done-that so what moment just like my little sisters

Their eleven between them waving at my two an echo of Ma Kelly on our avenue her

Seventeen pregnancies paraded regularly at our ma's paltry three and was he her son

Still her son though she had heard him clearly calling on His Father from the cross but a

Mother is a mother a Jewish mother surely so a visit home before His ascension to His

Source His heavenly home ah there we have it a pattern emerging of birth life death and

Resurrection to a heavenly home Christ's journey surely and as
   believer also mine and
Dara's also then of course so both of us you to your earthly
   father the pair of us in our
Final heavenly home together there together.

Then, Now, Next 2

Happy birthday to you
Happy birthday to you
Happy Birthday dear Dara
Happy birthday to you so

Yes and yet another would have been day these celebrations of
your birth melding and
Merging time and even space as I recall last Christmas in Dub-
lin and your big brother's
Fiftieth and in my mind already then today your forty eighth
the difference in knowing
Him a pink wizened wrinkled creature in an incubator all the
way through three
Countries his adolescence teens and early manhood to a mildly
chubby bearded married
Man in Dublin of all places my hometown and you still becom-
ing who you might have
Been when the wandering pilgrim reaper harvested your barely
teenage soul the chaff of
Your body burnt to ash long washed away in a Swedish garden
of remembrance so your
Birthday a reminder of who you were and not yet not yet were
as if I was waiting for
You later on a later on which never came for either of us ever
not even maybe now who
Knows not I though maybe you with your sardonic knowall
teenage smile of then and
Then I mean before you died may have figured it all out as you
often did by now and

Even wonder what the fuck I'm going on about and if you're out
    there somewhere in
Some or another form then you or the what of you will know
    I'm reaching out to you
Then now next you my ultimate anam cara the energy inform-
    ing and organising this my
End of a journey suite the route now known the meaning now
    revealed finally revealed.

EPILOGUE

Downsizing

Not something I expected really ageing I mean mine of course
  its attendant ills like
COPD diabetes blocked arteries TIAs my prostate enlarging
  itself then cancerous so
Surgeries biopsies and other invasive procedures and peeing and
  shitting myself from
All of the foregoing its medications often adding cause effect
  and variation all
Covered already so moving on or going forward as we now seem
  to be saying to
Movements of another sort of me not in and out of me me see-
  ing the writing on the
Wall of life mine I mean of course time to let go go forward of
  course start leaving all I
Had accumulated adding nothing first to go my lovely two be-
  doom top floor apartment
Library bookcases and all in a dumpster as I exchanged for a
  one bedroom halfway up
Or down maybe in the same building so changed apartment
  though barely address so
Fourth floor now from eighthth a downwards move a lot of
  space in many ways to less
Less also to hold now only essentials my music and their Billys
  chairs sofa and a desk to
Work on a kitchen table from a friend the previous table now
  my desk only an accidental
Table by default and anyway I'm wandering having moved from
  ageing and mortality to

Actual dying and death so no more me an end also to my com-
   mentary on being me the
Phases of my fading a photo losing focus on the figure in the
   lens as background emerges
Mortality in general now mine in particular from general theme
   to personal reality my
Death in fact not any longer a philosophical reflection so join-
   ing soon enough I feel the
Monty Python parrot my final downsizing from two bedrooms
   to one and then to my
Final removal a one-room apartment made for burning or burial
   as my parish priest
Pater Dominic decides for a corpse no longer me nor mine...

Who me?

Difficult to imagine no longer being when the imaginer is me a
  prawn sandwich and a
Sauvignon Blanc before me typing about going forward after
  ageing and downsizing to a
Coffin for the remains of who I used to be the final what of me
  before the worms or
Flames did their thing a skeleton or ashes neither of which can
  enjoy a glass taste a
Sandwich or type a word or line or even think about how it is to
  be a skeleton ashes
Really truly to no longer be me in this world anyway and hardly
  any rows of robot MACs
Soul-steered where I hope to go with mercy and a good word or
  two my angels and my
Anam cara nudge nudge wink wink a prayer or two and we'll
  kinda sorta meet again so
That's my issue not able to experience reflect on put words to
  no longer being who I was
Have been and am now as I write of no longer being the me I
  knew know leave behind
Wave farewell to though he me has no longer anywhere to go a
  no-one nowhere in a
No man's land between life and death and actually dying me
  doing a Heidegger and
Sartre in real time if even in my head though existential I can
  promise you existential...

The Waiting Room

I mean what else is there to do here here in death's waiting
  room but wait so okay okay

Read I suppose my Kindle primed and loaded though let's be
  serious write reviews in

My odd unpunctuated verse as metaphorical kindling for my
  hellish exit and my writing

More and more my main concern since Las Meninas so finally
  my focus back where it

Was in my stammering teens a writer of poetry more than a
  poet perhaps and in itself a

Deflection from maybe finally accepting here on my metaphori-
  cal deathbed a future

Membership of the dead poets' society who knows not I and
  not my claim to make in my

Traditional Anglo Irish world where poet is an honour bestowed
  and not a title lightly

Self-conferred so there you have it there you have it though not
  I no still not I can't say it

With conviction I'm a poet so fuck it maybe I'm not though
  fuck it fuck it maybe I just am

A poet though he doesn't know it as the mother of a former
  girlfriend once called me to

My great shortlived delight though didn't impress the girlfriend
  neither then nor after

40 years my sixtieth in Dublin all the way from Stockholm an
  exile returned and singing

A song I wrote at the time I knew her which only reminded her
  of another former

Boyfriend so still an also ran who knew it then and later then
  again though back to my

Discovered or uncovered theme it seems as always emerging in
    the unplanned dynamic
My writing encourages out of the shell of me my oceans sound-
    ing in my ear becoming
Words and lines and okay fuck it poems however odd still po-
    ems so maybe the laddie
Doth protest too much me I mean of course me of course who
    else me in my well hidden
Shyness hiding now again as I notice the Swenglish intruding
    now again gently of course
Gently as my 44 years here peep through my Irishness and
    career here as a teacher of
English up to my entry into therapy first as client then trainee
    and then practitioner then
Academia offered me a floppy hat and gown welcomed and
    worn with quiet satisfaction
Always and still a quiet satisfaction my doctor's hat and gown
    donated with my other
Unused clothing to a charity so if you see a homeless man in
    Stockholm looking doctoral
English style it is a case of there but for the grace of God go I
    so give him some kronor in
My name Seán a poet though he only got to know it if he ever
    did not long before he died.

The Pilgrim Reaper

Remembering a favourite line of mine from my youth about
 infections that were

Concordeing it around the globe and now the Concorde dead as
 the dodo and as

Airlines bankrupt slowly into dodohood or worse for us takeo-
 vers hospice mergers the

Blind not only leading the blind the dying giving the kiss of
 death to the dying our

Acquired faith in the economy tested to the limits of of its
 meaning and naturally

Found wanting so it's maybe not the economy stoopid but the
 stoopid economy our

Secular chickens coming home to roost having lost not only
 their religion but worse

Freedom of thought a personal philosophy borrowed bought
 into or uniquely theirs so

Cures found plenteous with pills their producers and purveyors
 their market shares

Profits and dividends statistics in the graveyards of the dead our
 next and next and

Next generations so maybe lemmings we've become our quanti-
 ty and impact more than

Even we can bear and more than the world we live in can toler-
 ate without response so a

Virus emerges which can kill us and save us the dilemma of
 personal submission to

Mass suicide with each of us an anybody and a nobody two for
 the price of none the

Virus our pilgrim reaper walking to a Santiago to save our world
first cleaning it of the
Poison of our presence and then perhaps of us ourselves and so
a vacant freehold for
Passersby or some remnants of us who had understood a thing
or two about life on
Earth our earth our home our place in the complex scheme of
things I'll never know so
Dead by age ailments or virus no longer anyway here so happy
that I care...

Bag in Box

That's me I suppose the bag now drained a squish perhaps
dropping on an early Risotto

Always a favourite since my time in Milano and Sabri and Davide's visit to Stockholm

Complete with porcini and home made risotto ai porcini a
Venetian red of course and

Great company shared memories of Dublin and Lydders so
Dublin my sister her son my

Composer nephew Lydders' da and Vicenza of course before I
got there Lydders'

Birthday new strings for her violin bow after a stroll through
the Palladian city its rivers

Bridges and squares our pally chat and a spritzer in town with
passerby Pietro poor lad

Ciao ciao bambino and me now wondering where the meaning
of my metaphors is

Hiding could it maybe be in plain sight of course it is there
already in my first two words

That's me a coloured box of recycled cardboard with an empty
plastic bag once full with

Anyway half decent Chenin Blanc with this my almost squeezed
final squish drop of an

Almost downer almost and let's face it a half decent Chenin
Blanc could never be a

Gently chilled Sancerre or New Zealand Sauvignon blanc even
so maybe I could consider

Burying or burning the box after I've drained these maybe final
drops from me as bag a

Dress rehearsal for my pale corpse the bag of me now empty of
all words waste plastic?

August 9, 2020

So here we are again son your
Death day now as then a mere 3 months after your
Birth day me still celebrating you in me on both of them me
Keeping no not your memory keeping you the person you Dara
    you
Alive still in this world with me as long as I'm still here and
    then we'll see so
Yes and then we'll see your oh so simple message to me this
    time then we'll see.